HOW SMART ARE YOU?

What's Your I.Q.?

DR. PAMELA A. HORN

Self-Scoring Test to Discover Your
Aptitude and Intelligence
for Children and Adults

Calculate Your I.Q. in Seconds with
the I.Q. Scoring Chart

Questions and Answers Compiled Under
the Direction of the
Chelsea Education Institution

Sweetwater Press

Printed in Canada

ISBN: 1-40371-187-9

10 9 8 7 6 5 4 3 2 1

Dr. Pamela A. Horn is a lawyer, author, book publisher editor and student of games of logic. She earned a Bachelor of Arts degree at Carnegie Mellon University in Pittsburgh, Pennsylvania, and a Juris Doctor at Cardozo Law School in New York City.

This self-scoring test is not intended for clinical use and in no way can replace, simulate, or substitute for I.Q. testing administered by a qualified professional psychologist. If you wish to pursue a definitive I.Q. analysis, consult a qualified professional psychologist.

1. PYRAMID is to TRIANGLE as SPHERE is to:

   a. UNIVERSE b. CIRCLE   c. ARC
   d. RADIUS   e. CURVE

2. Which does not belong?

   a. MOGUL   b. GO-BETWEEN
   c. DISTRIBUTOR   d. BROKER
   e. AGENT

3. Which word has two familiar homo-phones (words that sound alike but are different in meaning and spelling)?

   a. SHOOT   b. THREW   c. FLUE
   d. DRAW   e. TAIL

4. SILK is to FABRIC as MUTTON is to

   a. SHEEP   b. RACK   c. MEAT
   d. CHOP   e. LAMB

5. What is the missing number in this series?

   73, 12, 6, 3, 5, ___, 4, 4

   a. 10   b. 55   c. 6
   d. 20   e. 4

6. Jack is 18 years old, three times as old as his sister Tara. In how many years will Tara be half as old as Jack is now?

   a. 2   b. 3   c. 4
   d. 5   e. 6

7. What is the missing picture?

a.   b.   c.

d.   e.

3

8. John works four blocks north and four blocks east from his home. By only going north and/or east, how many different ways can John walk to work?

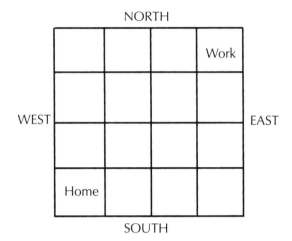

9. What follows next?

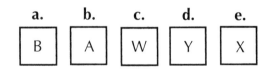

10. Find the missing number.

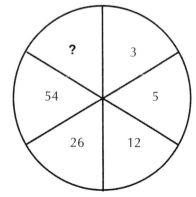

a. 86   b. 96   c. 110   d. 124   e. 142

11. What three letters can you add to each of the letters below that will make words?
ch...
cl...
d...
tr...
st...
v...

12. What three letters can you add to each of the letters below that will make words?
b...
sp...
resp...
qu...
term...
s...

13. Which anagram does not belong?

a. TOGA   b. KEDYON   c. EPHES
d. OSHUE   e. ORESH

14. Which picture follows next in the sequence?

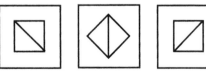

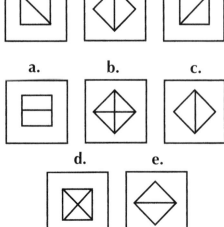

4

15. Which figure belongs next in the sequence?

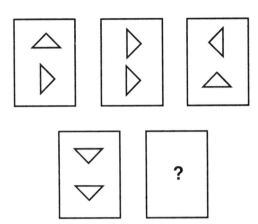

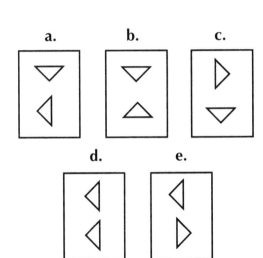

16. Which word would mean the opposite if you changed the last three letters to BLE?

    a. CONSIDERATE   b. HORRIFIC
    c. TANKS d. STAIRS e. TERRIFIC

17. Which one is <u>least</u> like the rest?

    a. HOUSE   b. QUARTERS
    c. NURSING HOME d. CHURCH
    e. ABODE

18. If OPEN equals 50, what does CLOSED equal?

    a. 100   b. 17   c. 58   d. 6   e. 79

19. Which is the odd one out?

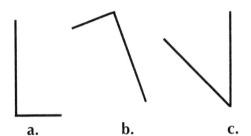

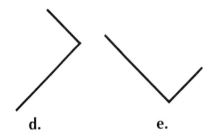

20. If Christmas Eve is on a Thursday, which anagram is the day on which Martin Luther King Jr. Day is observed the following year?

    a. DIFRAY   b. DYNAMO
    c. RHUDASTY   d. STEAYUD
    e. RUDYASTA

21. Which word is most opposite of AFFLUENCE?

    a. WHIMSY   b. EBULLIENCE
    c. POVERTY   d. CONFLUENCE
    e. INFERIORITY

22. Which of the following does not belong?

    a. FLUTE b. BANJO   c. GUITAR
    d. HARP   e. BASS

23. ◯ is to ▢ as ▢ is to what?

    a. ◯   **b.** ▢

    c. ◯   **d.** ▢

    e. NONE OF THESE

24. If Jennifer has PANACHE, she has…

    a. A ROSY COMPLEXION b. HUMOR
    c. A FEVER d. FLAIR e. LETHARGY

25. STUDIO is to DANCE as MOSQUE is to:

    a. MOSLEM b. WORSHIP
    c. CHURCH d. DOME   e. FAITH

26. What is the next word in the sequence?

    BASE   MINOR   USAGE

    a. END   b. OLDER   c. TOP
    d. UNIT   e. IRON

27. Which does not belong?

    a. SWITZERLAND b. ETHIOPIA
    c. MADAGASCAR d. SICILY
    e. MOROCCO

28. WINDOW is to SHADE as EYE is to:

    a. LASH   b. LID c. BROW
    d. PUPIL   e. NOSE

29. Choose the best synonym for PLIANT:

    a. FLEXIBLE   b. MUSCULAR
    c. STRINGENT   d. STRIDENT
    e. GRIPPING

30. Which does not belong?

    a. KANGAROO   b. SNAKE
    c. ELEPHANT   d. CENTIPEDE
    e. ANT

31. WAVE is to WATER as ZEPHYR is to:

    a. HARP   b. RAIN   c. DUST
    d. AIR   e. MUSIC

32. Four different colored tables are placed in a row. The blue table is next to the green table but not next to the red. The red table is not next to the yellow. Which table is next to the yellow?

    a. BLUE   b. GREEN   c. RED
    d. NOT ENOUGH INFORMATION
       TO DETERMINE

33. Which is the odd one out?

    a. SKIRT   b. PANTS   c. BAG
    d. HAT   e. STOCKINGS

34. ROW BOAT is to OAR as AUTOMOBILE is to:

    a. IGNITION   b. ENGINE   c. OIL
    d. GASOLINE   e. SPARK PLUG

35. Which is the odd one out?

    a.   **b.**

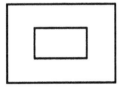

    c.   **d.**

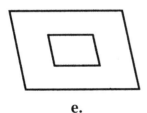

    e.

36. Which word is the best antonym for CONCAVE?

    a. STRAIGHT   b. FULL
    c. VACUOUS   d. BULGING
    e. ABOVE

37. Choose the word with the same meaning as ARTIFICE.

    a. TALE   b. ELEMENT
    c. PAINTING   d. INNOCENCE
    e. CUNNING

38. Which is the odd one out?

    a. TREE   b. MANGO
    c. SHRUB   d. BUSH
    e. HEDGE

39. Which is the missing figure?

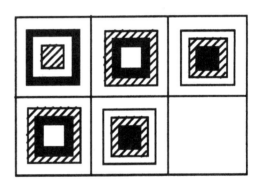

    a.   **b.**   **c.**

    d.   **e.**

40. If ATLANTIC equals 80, PACIFIC equals what?

    a. 47   b. 40   c. 32
    d. 160   e. 71

41. Which does not belong?

a. BASKET   b. SATCHEL
c. GLOVE   d. BUCKET
e. PURSE

42. What do you get if you unscramble
these letters?
"UECADRO"

a. A RIVER   b. A CITY
c. A STATE   d. A COUNTRY
e. AN OCEAN

43. Choose the best synonym for
CONNOISSEUR:

a. PROTAGONIST   b. ANTAGONIST
c. PEDESTRIAN   d. NEGOTIATOR
e. EXPERT

44. The customer asked the shopkeeper,
"How much does this bag of apples
weigh?" The shopkeeper replied,
"Two-thirds of its weight plus three
and one-third pounds." How much
did the bag of apples weigh?

a. 6 lbs.   b. 8 lbs.   c. 9 lbs.
d. 10 lbs.   e. 12 lbs.

45. BRUSH is to PAINTER as SHEARS
are to:

a. MASON   b. GARDENER
c. ARTIST   d. ARCHITECT
e. WRITER

46. Sally and her mother returned from
the store with 24 packages. Sally's
mother parked the car 80 feet from
their house. Sally's mother can carry
three packages at a time, but Sally
can carry only two. How many feet
do they have to walk together to
take all the packages into the
house? They both took the same
number of trips.

a. 720 ft.
b. 800 ft.
c. 1,280 ft.
d. 1,440 ft.
e. 1,600 ft.

47. Which word does not belong?

a. ROOM   b. DOG   c. BOOK
d. DEER   e. TORT   f. SAW

48. If Gash = 8291, Twin = 6743, and
No = 35,

who is 7291438653?

49. Which word does not belong?

a. ASSORTMENT   b. PASTICHE
c. UNIFORMITY   d. MÉLANGE
e. POTPOURRI

50. Which does not belong?

a. FRANCE   b. NETHERLANDS
c. SPAIN   d. SWEDEN
e. UNITED KINGDOM

51. Which comes next in this sequence?

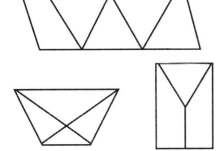

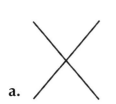

a.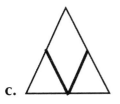
b.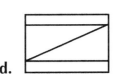

c.
d.

e.

52. Which is the odd word out?

a. DILL   b. CIVIL   c. MILL
d. MIND   e. LIVID   f. MIX
g. DIM

53. Which does not belong?

a. FRUGAL   b. PARSIMONIOUS
c. CONFIDENT   d. NIGGARDLY
e. SPARING

54. Subtract the square of the fourth lowest number from the third highest even number.

6	24	80	5	17	14	1
72	11	56	30	4	12	10
41	2	96	50	29	31	7

a. 35   b. 36   c. 44
d. 47   e. 60

55. OAK is to TREE as CHERRY is to:

a. SEED   b. FRUIT
c. PLANT   d. VEGETABLE
e. FLOWER

56. What is the best synonym for GRIPE?

a. BULLY   b. RAGE
c. GRIEVANCE   d. SOLUTION
e. PACIFY

57. 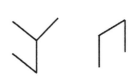 is to as is to

a. **b.** **c.**

d. **e.**

9

58. Kate is three times as old as Spencer, Molly is half as old as Samantha, and Samantha is three years older than Kate. If Spencer is five years old, how old is Molly?

   a. EIGHT   b. NINE   c. TEN
   d. ELEVEN   e. TWELVE

59. Which is the odd one out?

   a. STREET   b. GUTTER   c. SEWER
   d. CURB   e. AWNING

60. What is the next figure?

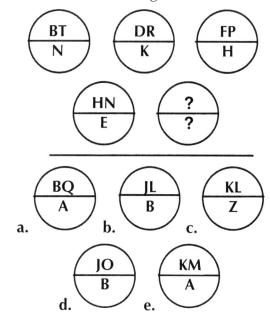

a.   b.   c.

d.   e.

61. COW is to CALF as GOAT is to:

   a. GANDER   b. SOW   c. KID
   d. PUP   e. GULLET

62. Which is the odd one out?

   a. LITER   b. YARD   c. ACRE
   d. METER   e. INCH

63. KIMONO is to DRESS as KILT is to:

   a. COAT   b. HABIT   c. SLACKS
   d. SKIRT   e. CAPE

64. What does not belong?

   a. CRAB   b. LOBSTER c. SKATE
   d. CLAM   e. SHRIMP

65. Which one comes next?

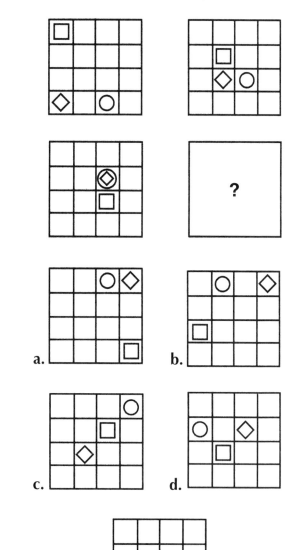

66. Which figure is next?

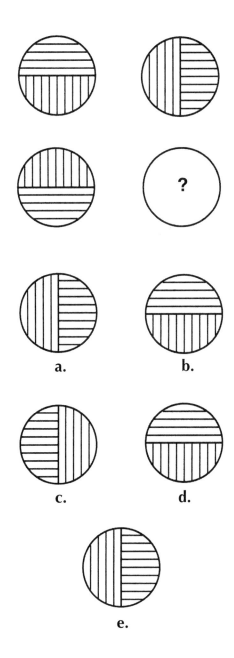

a.

b.

c.

d.

e.

67. If you rearrange the letters WEEDARLA, what do you get?

    a. A RIVER   b. A CITY
    c. A COUNTRY d. A PLANET
    e. A CONTINENT

68. What comes next in this sequence?

a.   b.

c.

d.   e.

69. A hand is four inches long from the base of the palm to its fingertips. The measurement of the upper arm (elbow to the shoulder) is the same as the hand plus one-third the size of the forearm (wrist to the elbow). The forearm (wrist to the elbow) is the size of the hand plus five inches. What is the length from the fingertips to the shoulder?

    a. 18 INCHES   b. 20 INCHES
    c. 22 INCHES   d. 24 INCHES
    e. 26 INCHES

70. If all X's are Y's and all Y's are Z's, then all X's are definitely Z's. This statement is:

a. TRUE   b. FALSE
c. NOT ENOUGH INFORMATION

71. What is the best antonym for MELLIFLUOUS?

a. MUSICAL   b. FLUID
c. RAUCOUS   d. SMOOTH
e. SOFT

72. If STOP equals 70 then START equals what?

a. 80   b. 56   c. 74
d. 78   e. 83

73. Which figure is least like the other four?

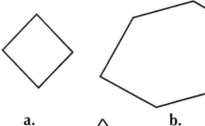

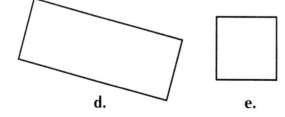

a.   b.

c.

d.   e.

74. Which domino is next?

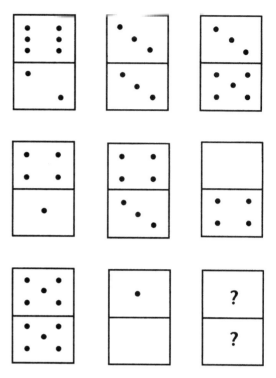

75. Which card is next?

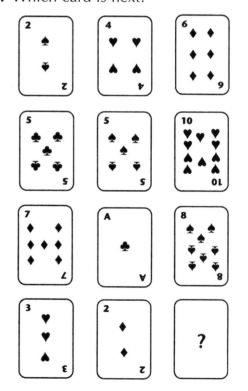

12

76. VENDOR is to CONSUMER as RESTAURATEUR is to:

    a. WAITER   b. PATRON
    c. WHOLESALER   d. DEALER
    e. CHEF

77. Which does not belong?

    a. HAIL   b. RECEIVE
    c. WELCOME   d. SHUN
    e. ACCEPT

78. What should the last number in the series be?

    2,   10,   5,   13,   8,   16,
    11, 19, 14, 22,   ?

    a. 17   b. 13   c. 19
    d. 14   e. 24

79. What is the best synonym for HARVEST?

    a. PLANT   b. SOW   c. COLLECT
    d. SEED   e. FALL

80. What comes next?

    16   XIX   25   XXXVII
    61   ?

    a. CIV
    b. 120
    c. 112
    d. CIX
    e. CXXIV

I.Q. ANSWERS

1. b. CIRCLE. A PYRAMID is a three dimensional TRIANGLE, and a SPHERE is a three dimensional CIRCLE.

2. a. MOGUL. All the other choices are mediators or middle people.

3. c. FLUE (Flu & Flew). FLUE is the only choice with two homophones.

4. c. MEAT. SILK is a type of FABRIC and MUTTON is a type of MEAT.

5. e. 4. Each number, starting with twelve, states the number of letters in the preceeding number.

6. b. 3. Jack is 18, three times as old as Tara who must be 6. It will be 3 years until Tara turns 9 years old, which is half as old as Jack is now.

7. d. The first figure is placed under the second.

8. There are twenty routes that John can travel to work from home by going only north and/or east. Figure it out for yourself.

9. d. Y is the answer because G is the fourth letter after C, L is the fifth letter after G, R is the sixth letter after L, and Y is the seventh letter after R.

10. c. 110. The sequence is: add the previous numbers plus 2, then 4, then 6, then 8, then 10. That is:

    3
    3+2=5
    3+5+4=12
    3+5+12+6=26
    3+5+12+26+8=54
    3+5+12+26+54+10=110

11. AMP. Champ, clamp, damp, tramp, stamp, vamp.

12. ITE. Bite, spite, respite, quite, termite, site.

13. d. OSHUE. OSHUE is an anagram for house. All the others are anagrams for animals. TOGA is GOAT; KEDYON is DONKEY; EPHES is SHEEP; and ORESH is HORSE.

14. e. The square and the line intersecting two corners are both turning clockwise 90° at each stage.

15. a. The top figure rotates clockwise 90°, 180°, 270°, and then 360°. The bottom figure rotates clockwise 360°, 270°, 180°, and then 90°.

16. e. TERRI(FIC) – TERRI(BLE)

17. d. CHURCH. One doesn't live in a church but can live in a house, quarters, a nursing home, or an abode.

18. c. 58. If you assign number values to each letter in the alphabet, such as A=1, B=2, C=3, D=4, E=5, etc., then

O	P	E	N
15	16	5	14 = 50,

C	L	O	S	E	D
3	12	15	19	5	4 = 58.

19. c. All the other figures have two lines, one twice as long as the other. Answer (c) has two lines of equal size.

20. b. DYNAMO – "MONDAY"

21. c. POVERTY is the opposite of AFFLUENCE.

22. a. FLUTE. All the other choices are stringed instruments. A flute is a wind instrument.

23. c. The correct answer alternates the shape and the side that is dotted.

24. d. FLAIR. PANACHE means having FLAIR.

25. b. WORSHIP. A STUDIO is a place to DANCE, and a MOSQUE is a place to WORSHIP.

26. e. IRON. The sequence is:
    bAsE mInOr UsAgE IrOn

    A-E-I-O-U-A-E-I-O

27. d. SICILY. All other choices are countries. SICILY is part of a country, Italy.

28. b. LID. A SHADE covers a WINDOW and a LID covers an EYE.

29. a. FLEXIBLE. PLIANT means able to be bent.

30. b. SNAKE. All the others walk on legs except for the snake.

31. d. AIR. A WAVE is moving WATER, and a ZEPHYR is moving AIR.

32. a. BLUE. They would have to be YELLOW, BLUE, GREEN, RED.

33. c. BAG. This is the only article you don't wear on your body.

34. b. ENGINE. A ROWBOAT is propelled by an OAR, and an AUTOMOBILE is propelled by an ENGINE.

35. d. It is the only figure made with curved rather than straight lines.

36. d. BULGING. CONCAVE means curving into itself.

37. e. CUNNING.

38. b. MANGO. This is the fruit of a tree, the others are types of flora.

39. e. This figure completes the series. The pattern is that the outer square progresses to the second inner square, then to the third. The stripes begin in the outer square and end up in the center square.

40. a. 47.

A	T	L	A	N	T	I	C
1	20	12	1	14	20	9	3 = 80,

P	A	C	I	F	I	C
16	1	3	9	6	9	3 = 47.

41. c. GLOVE. All the other objects are used to carry things, and a glove is worn.

42. d. A COUNTRY – "ECUADOR"

43. e. EXPERT. CONNOISSEUR comes from the Latin "conoscere" or the French "connaître," to know.

44. d. 10 lbs. Create an equation from the shopkeeper's response where the total weight of the bag equals x. Then, $2x/3 + 3\ 1/3 = x$. When you solve the equation for x, you find the total weight of the bag is 10 lbs.

45. b. GARDENER

46. d. 1,440 ft. The two of them each walk 720 feet, making four round trips between the car and the house and one last trip from the car to the house.

47. c. BOOK. All the other words spell other words when spelled backward.

48. WASHINGTON. W=7, A=2, S=9, H=1, I=4, N=3, G=8, T=6, O=5, N=3

49. c. UNIFORMITY. All the other words are synonyms.

50. a. FRANCE. All the other countries currently have a monarch.

51. d. The sequence contains figures with the letters W, X, and Y in them. In order to complete the sequence, the next figure must contain Z.

52. d. MIND. All the other words have short i sounds. And all the other words are made up with Roman numerals. N is not a Roman numeral.

53. c. CONFIDENT. All the others are synonyms for one another.

54. d. 47. $72 - 5^2\ (25) = 47$

55. b. FRUIT. An OAK is a type of TREE, and a CHERRY is a type of FRUIT. CHERRY is also a tree, but that is not one of the suggested answers.

56. c. GRIEVANCE is the best synonym for GRIPE.

57. d. These lines complete the cube.

58. b. NINE. Spencer is five, Kate is 15, Samantha is 18, so Molly is 9.

59. e. AWNING. All the other choices are on the ground and an awning rises above the ground.

60. b. The sequence is: the first letter above is every other letter (B, D, F, H, J). The second letter above is every other letter going backward (T, R, P, N, L). The letter below is every third letter going backward (N, K, H, E, B).

61. c. KID. A CALF is a baby COW, and a KID is a baby GOAT.

62. a. LITER. Liter measures volume. All the others measure distance or area.

63. d. SKIRT. A KIMONO is a type of DRESS and a KILT is a type of SKIRT.

64. c. A SKATE is a fish and has no shell. The others all do.

65. a. The square moves diagonally from upper left to lower right. The diamond moves diagonally from lower left to upper right. The circle moves straight upward.

66. c. The circle turns 90° counter-clockwise each time.

67. a. A RIVER — "DELAWARE"

68. e. The number of dots in each figure is calculated by doubling the previous number of dots: 2, then 4, then 8, then 16 dots.

69. b. 20 INCHES. The hand is four inches, the forearm is nine inches, and the upper arm is seven inches.

70. a. TRUE. If you want, you can plug in actual classifications and see how the logic works: i.e., if all tigers are cats and all cats are animals, then all tigers are definitely animals.

71. c. RAUCOUS. MELLIFLUOUS means beautiful sounding and RAUCOUS describes a sound that is harsh and unpleasant.

72. d. 78. Assign each letter the value corresponding to its numerical placement in the alphabet, and add them up.

S	T	O	P	
19	20	15	16 = 70,	

S	T	A	R	T
19	20	1	18	20 = 78.

73. c. All but "c" have parallel sides. OR
b. All but "b" have equal-sized angles

74. The missing domino has 4 dots on the top and 5 dots below. For the upper half of the domino, the third number is the difference between the first and the second domino. For the lower half, the third number is the sum of the first two.

75. FIVE OF CLUBS. Add the first two cards to get the sum for the card on the right. The sequence of the suits left to right is spades, hearts, diamonds, clubs, spades, hearts, diamonds, clubs, etc.

76. b. PATRON. A CONSUMER buys from a VENDOR, and a PATRON buys from a RESTAURATEUR.

77. d. SHUN. SHUN is the opposite of all the other choices.

78. a. 17. The progression in the series is plus 8, minus 5, plus 8, minus 5, etc.

79. c. COLLECT. To HARVEST means to COLLECT.

80. d. CIX. The number should be a Roman numeral. Add 3 to first number and double the addendum each time you add.

$16 + (3) = 19 (XIX)$
$XIX (19) + (6) = 25$
$25 + (12) = 37 (XXXVII)$
$37 + (24) = 61 (LXI)$
$61 + (48) = 109 (CIX)$

SCORING CHART IS ON THE BACK COVER